Rail Runabout

A look at Northern Ireland Railways from 1975 to 2005

Sam Somerville

Colourpoint Books

Rail Runabout
A look at Northern Ireland Railways from 1975 to 2005

For Elizabeth

All rights reserved. No part of this publication may be reproduced, stored in a retrieval system or transmitted in any form or by any means, electronic, mechanical, photocopying, scanning, recording or otherwise, without the prior written permission of the copyright owners and publisher of this book.

6 5 4 3 2 1

© Sam Somerville and Colourpoint Books 2006

Designed by Colourpoint Books, Newtownards
Printed by: ColourBooks Ltd

ISBN 1 904242 64 2

Colourpoint Books
Colourpoint House
Jubilee Business Park
21 Jubilee Road
Newtownards
County Down
Northern Ireland
BT23 4YH
Tel: 028 9182 0505
Fax: 028 9182 1900
E-mail: info@colourpoint.co.uk
Web-site: www.colourpoint.co.uk

Sam Somerville has had an interest in railways since childhood. One of his earliest memories is travelling to Omagh on a steam train whilst a heavy blizzard was blowing in the Sperrins. His interest nowadays includes light rail and buses. Sam has travelled throughout Europe studying and photographing various forms of transport. Educated at the University of Ulster, he is married and lives in Carrickfergus, Co Antrim.

This is his first book.

Unless otherwise credited all photographs are by the author.

Front cover: An 80 class set, led by No 82, departs from Portrush on a summer Saturday, while two Leyland Tigers and a Bristol RE rest in the adjacent Ulsterbus yard. A Railway Preservation Society of Ireland 'Portrush Flyer' steam special, hauled by preserved GNR 4-4-0 No 85 *Merlin*, awaits departure from platform 3.

Rear cover: Hunslet No 102 *Falcon* propels its five-coach Belfast Central to Londonderry train north on the Lisburn to Antrim line.

Introduction
Rail Runabout

The theme for this fourth volume in the 'Irish Railway Photographers' series is a look back at thirty years of change on the main line railway system in Northern Ireland. I make no claim that the photographs chosen represent all that some readers might deem important but I do feel they properly represent Northern Ireland Railways (NIR) in the period under review. Not until the selection process is under way does one identify where the strengths and weaknesses of a collection might lie. In my case, there was a shortage of photographs of NIR General Motors locos Nos 208 and 209 in NIR blue, arguably the more attractive of the two liveries these machines have carried.

The photographs I've chosen are as much about a period of change in Northern Ireland as they are about railways. Railways exist for a reason and are not in a vacuum. Many readers of this book will already know the history of the MPD (multi-purpose diesel) railcars and that the MED (multi-engined diesel) units spent most of their life on the Bangor line. It is not my intention to repeat this information but would, instead, refer the reader to Colm Flanagan's *Diesel Dawn* (Colourpoint 2003).

My observation of the 'Save Our Railways' campaign during 2000 and into 2001 led me to conclude that in spite of the validity of the argument offered, there was also a lot of nonsense talked by those whose attachment to rail lacked any understanding of the realities of rail economics. On account of this, and given the lack of a definitive history of bus and rail services in Northern Ireland since the formation of the Ulster Transport Authority in 1948 to the present day, I have, within the very limited space an introduction allows, attempted to place the photographs of the past thirty years within a more inclusive context.

The title of this volume comes from the NIR 'Rail Runabout' tickets that I, from about the age of ten, used to travel all over the NIR railway system, and also to Dundalk. Memories, such as travelling from Waterside goods yard in Derry to Portrush on an eleven coach empty stock transfer train (steam-hauled, of course), of ex-GNR enginemen from Great Victoria Street station letting young enthusiasts such as myself travel up front on runs to and from Lisburn, or the tales the late Gerry Eadie, stationmaster at Finaghy, or drivers Andy Rushe and Bobby Quail, would come out with, remain strong.

I have no idea how many tickets I bought during the period 1966 to the late 1980s but it must have been dozens. Memories and echoes of years past still resonate at certain places today but whilst the railway is still there, the magic and spirit has left it. Clinical-like efficiency is the new culture on NIR.

I trust anyone who takes a look at the photographs in the book will enjoy whatever memories they bring as much as I did looking back on them.

A young Sam Somerville in the cab of a Córas Iompair Éireann (CIÉ) General Motors locomotive at Dundalk on 9 September 1967. *Jim Edgar*

NORTHERN IRELAND RAILWAYS
(STANDARD CLASS)

RAIL A 0066
RUNABOUT

SEVEN DAYS UNLIMITED TRAVEL TICKET

Not Transferable
Name: MR SOMERVILLE
VALID FROM Day: THURSDAY UNTIL WEDNESDAY
Date: 14TH APRIL 1988 UNTIL 20TH APRIL 1988
(BOTH DATES INCLUSIVE)

This ticket entitles the holder named above subject to the Conveyance of Passengers Conditions, to unlimited travel by the Company's timetable train services (Standard Class) which operate between stations within Northern Ireland.

HOLDER'S SIGNATURE
(SEE REVERSE SIDE FOR MAP)

A R.R. 0066 CHILD
FARE £

The thirty years of change has been comprehensive and not only is the reformed railway different in a physical way but the old railway culture, rooted in the steam era, has all but died. That is not a bad thing in itself as the railway, in all facets, has to move in line with change in wider society. But in the process it seems to have become slave to an over-administered, over-regulated and politically correct culture. This can only result in sapping the residue of the spirit that made railway employees, in May 1967, strike in support of their Managing Director, dismissed for saying he was not in place to administer the last rites to the Northern Ireland railway system.

The physical change is very evident to anyone comparing the railway in 1975 with that of today. For myself as a photographer, I miss the clutter of the old railway – station furniture, semaphore signals and the telegraph pole lines which remind me of childhood trips with my family to Omagh. The Derry Road from Portadown had huge telegraph poles with perhaps up to 30 wires fixed to them. To a six-year-old, they symbolised the importance of the now lost link to the west. Those of you with an eagle eye might still see one on the disused embankment not far from the M1 motorway, about three miles southeast of Dungannon.

Whilst the physical change was an important element of renewal, those of you whose interest runs deep will understand that all was not as portrayed. The AD Little report in March 2000 laid bare, in no uncertain terms, the extent of the need for comprehensive renewal if the railway was not to drift towards becoming a worn out and antediluvian relic for which closure of the greater part would be the only realistic option.

The debate which followed the AD Little report, the 'Save Our Railways' campaign organised by the *Belfast Telegraph* newspaper and the favourable political and media opinion to the significance of retaining the railway system in its entirety, has been reflected by a more pro active effort by operator Translink to recast the railway to enable and equip it to meet the growing demand that rail travel is experiencing. This *will* continue in Northern Ireland if the economic foundations of the Province are rebuilt and railway investment continues.

Central to the efforts of Translink are the 23 new Spanish-built diesel multiple units which entered service in 2004/5. The size of the order for these stylish, new trains was the biggest ever for railways in Northern Ireland. Whilst welcome, there is a shortfall in the number required to fully deliver a new rail service throughout the Province. They do, however, represent both a vote of confidence and work in progress.

A fleet of new trains, the primary routes chosen to employ them on and even the title 'new inspired rail service' used by Translink echoes back to some of the recommendations of the *Benson Report* of 1963. Then, as now, railway closures were in the news and in spite of the recent developments, the lines to Londonderry and Larne remain in a state of limbo. The Department for Regional Development (DRD), refuse to fund, in the long term, with other stake holders if required, the only rail link to Northern Ireland's second largest centre of population and the fourth largest city on the island of Ireland. And where else in the UK would the rail link to a town [Larne] requiring a vote of confidence in its economy, and an integral part of the EU-classified Trans European Network be threatened with closure?

Railways have no special right to exist, any more than any other aspect of the transport network and argument did exist for closures in the post-war years and may still do in rural parts of Great Britain.

But there are no rural lines left open for passenger traffic in Northern Ireland. The appearance as such of the Derry line has a direct correlation to severe, safety-related, limited expenditure on that line rather than investment reflective of the potential offered by the route and the demographics and political sensitivities of the area it serves.

The economic realities that Northern Ireland must face in the years ahead may not, from the narrow and rather parochial perspective of the DRD, seem to hold out much hope for the lines they consider 'non core'. Such a view, if realised, will be forgetful of one of the factors that led to the breakdown of society as the Troubles tore the heart out of Northern Ireland in the late 1960s and throughout the 1970s and 1980s.

The Campaign for Social Justice was strongly focused on issues in Co Tyrone in the years prior the outbreak of the Troubles. Its focus on social issues surrounding either real or perceived discrimination by the Stormont government towards the area west of the Bann ran concurrent with the last months of the railway linking Portadown and Londonderry via Omagh, which closed in February 1965 following acceptance by Stormont of the recommendations of the *Benson Report*. Sir Henry Benson (later Lord Benson), a leading accountant with Coopers and Lybrand, recalled in his autobiography many years later that he felt Stormont wanted him to recommend railway closure but was not formally told.

The impact of closure on the simmering time bomb that belied the optimistic and hopeful outlook of the 'swinging sixties' was implied in a speech by Sheelagh Murnaghan, Liberal MP for Queen's University and a native of Omagh, at Stormont on 2 June 1964. The closure of the railway from Portadown to Derry would, she said, ". . . be a serious mistake, one which they [the Northern Ireland Government] and Northern Ireland as a whole will have cause to regret in the future." The line closed and the rest, as they say, is history. Not to learn from that and still threaten the closure of the last rail link to the largest centre of population and most important city, not only west of the Bann but in the entire northwest of Ireland, might be construed as playing with fire.

The environmental debate is also changing completely the wider issues relevant to the future of railways. The DRD seems to be locked into a myopic mindset, setting out the future of the Northern Ireland economy as car and road dependent. That cars and an improved road system have no role to play is profound rubbish. Equally so, the present rail system has an important role to play as environmental issues become more important, possibly justifying the restoration of a few long closed routes. I have no doubt that the benefits of such reopenings would outweigh the investment and capital costs.

The aforementioned uncertainty over the routes to Larne and Londonderry, land use policy and the proposal to build a national sports stadium outside Lisburn, adjacent to the M1 motorway, rather than in Belfast, illustrates the depth of the DRD love affair with cars and roads, despite platitudes to the contrary.

It is a love affair that must be ended if the evidence from a wide range of scientific sources is to be believed. Oil reserves are dwindling and the limited success of alternative fuels means that transport planning cannot be insulated from externalities outside the Province, a process that not even the polished spin from the DRD can hide.

Is the Department for Regional Development as divorced from the unsettling message from worldwide scientific opinion as Stormont was over forty years previously to the simmering discontent that led to the events that left an impression on every family in Northern Ireland? I hope not. The wider societal benefits of rail embrace social and political realities and bring added value to the quality of life. To destroy that would be an act of madness.

Selected References:
Benson, Sir Henry, *Benson Report*, 1963
Hansard, Stormont, 2 June 1964
Internal NIR Report, *Economics and Operation of the Midland and North Western Region*, 1971

Arthur, Paul, *Government and Politics of Northern Ireland*, Longman 1980
Benson, The Lord, *Accounting for Life*, Kogan Page, 1989
Monopolies and Mergers Commission, *Report into NIR*, 1990
Roberts, Paul, *The End of Oil*, Bloomsbury, 2004

Acknowledgements:
I am extremely grateful to Norman Johnston and Paul Savage at Colourpoint Books for turning my text and photographs into this splendid book. I would also like to acknowledge the assistance of Martin Baumann for supplying data concerning scrap and disposal dates. Thanks, too, to Sammy Norton from Dunmurry for keeping the spirit of the GNR alive.

This September 1977 view shows a multi-purpose diesel (MPD) set, headed by No 45, at Waterside station in Londonderry. The central part of the once-attractive station frontage area had been destroyed in a bomb attack two years previously. The station closed, with services transferred to a new facility closer to the double-deck Craigavon Bridge, in 1980. No 45 was withdrawn in 1978, having served the Ulster Transport Authority and Northern Ireland Railways for nineteen years.

Notwithstanding the impact of the bomb attack on the station, rail services continued, with the station and the operating end of things running as normal. In this picture, an 80 Class set is preparing to leave with an afternoon train to Belfast. Trailer No 770, shown here, was destroyed by fire in September 1979 just three months after this view was captured. The gentleman with his back to the camera is shunter Johnny Sweeney, who formerly worked at the GNR station at Foyle Road.

Another 1979 picture up at the Maiden City shows CIÉ General Motors loco No 171, which had arrived earlier on a rare daytime freight overload from Dundalk, resting in the goods yard as a Belfast train leaves. Most freight at this time ran overnight, with a pair of 70 Class power cars, or sometimes a Hunslet locomotive, providing the traction. At the time of writing (March 2006) No 171 remains in service as the station pilot at Dundalk.

A sad reflection of the thinking towards the railway in Derry is the basic railway atmosphere in this 1989 view of 80 Class No 97 *Glenshesk* at the new station opened nine years earlier. By this stage, freight traffic was almost a memory. No 97, new in June 1978 and shown here in NIR InterCity livery of grey and blue with white, yellow and black stripes, was withdrawn in 2005.

This June 1978 view along the spectacular coastline near Downhill shows the annual May or June weedkilling train returning from Derry. Weedkilling activities on NIR today are undertaken at night by a rail/road vehicle, but for many years the NIR system was treated by the CIÉ train, shown here with 201 Class loco No 210.

Built by BREL Derby in 1981 as a demonstrator numbered RDB 977020, this vehicle came to NIR in 1982. It never carried an NIR number, being known simply as the Railbus. Travelling on it on a stormy night in the early 1980s leaving Portrush was almost as frightening as travelling on it on the occasion when the emergency brake was applied as a buckled rail came closer. As a student, I recall many trips on this vehicle. On one occasion, I decided to travel from Londonderry to Belfast using the Ulsterbus route 273 and saw the Railbus in Waterside station waiting to form the next train in the Belfast direction. As that service on a Friday would have perhaps 150 people on board leaving Derry, I was confident my decision to look out for the disused Derry Road rail bridges between Omagh and Strabane from a bus was the right one. The Railbus is seen here on a railtour at Downhill in 1989. It was withdrawn in 1993 but may now be seen on the Downpatrick Railway.

Nowadays a photograph such as this, and some others in this volume, would be impossible to take as track walking permits are no longer obtainable and Translink, and the courts, will, quite properly, deal severely with any example of trespass on railway lines. Here we see 70 Class No 76 *River Inver* heading west between the two tunnels outside Castlerock on a Belfast to Derry train. The second vehicle on this train is No 727, a former GNR vehicle built in 1943 and later converted to a buffet car. It was rebuilt as an Open Standard in 1965. No 727 made her last journey shortly after this August 1980 view, while No 76 was withdrawn in 1984.

By spring 1989, freight on the Londonderry line was very infrequent and the operation of a daytime train was rare. When it did occur, various domestic or work arrangements were known to change! A quick dash to the fridge to get the spare film, fill the car up with petrol and a thought or two en route to road traffic conditions and the position of the sun was usually the story behind such photographs. Here we see GM loco No 113 *Belfast and Co Down* leaving Castlerock with a loaded fertiliser train bound for Derry.

The 70 Class sets epitomised the former NCC main line in the performance league tables as much as steam did such was their speed and reliability. Here we see another view of No 76 *River Inver*, this time heading a Belfast (York Road)-bound train into Castlerock in September 1975.

The long hot summer of 1976 is best remembered by the author for getting severe sunburn at Portrush! By that year, the performance of the MPD units was worse than poor. York Road yard was littered with failed or withdrawn sets and those that did run frequently overheated and, sometimes, even went on fire. Here we see No 49 at the rear of a Portrush branch train leaving Coleraine station in June of that year. De-engined in 1979 and converted to a loco-hauled coach, she was used on a few Hunslet-hauled football specials before withdrawal.

70 Class No 75 *River Maine* runs down from the halt at Dhu Varren towards the popular seaside resort of Portrush on a summer Saturday in August 1984. New in 1966, No 75 gave almost twenty years service, being withdrawn in 1986 after being vandalised. On withdrawal, the 70 class railcars were dumped at Crosshill Quarry, Co Antrim due to the presence of asbestos.

The chance to travel on a locomotive-hauled train on the Londonderry line comes very rarely. On one occasion in August 1997 a special to Portrush was so rostered, with the return working from the north coast resort shown here at Coleraine. Had circumstances been different, these very capable locomotives might have had a chance to deliver a service on the Londonderry line more in keeping with its main line status.

Shortly after the closure of Cullybackey station and loop in October 1976, 70 Class No 77 *River Braid* heads an up train through the deserted station. The CIÉ-liveried coach is a BUT Brake Third trailer built by the GNR and waiting collection by the Railway Preservation Society of Ireland. No 77 was withdrawn in 1986 but the GNR coach, No 114, was to see over twenty years further service. The station has since reopened (28 June 1982) but the signal cabin has been demolished.

Pictured at Ballymena station in summer 1985 are train guard Billy Brown (left) and driver James Anderson. Billy now drives trains for NIR whilst James is reputed to be enjoying his retirement in north Antrim. No 77 is now only a memory but it is thought her engine now powers 450 Class No 456 *Gosford Castle*.

One of the more interesting events in the period covered were the special trains that ran between Antrim and Muckamore, about 1½ miles east of Antrim on the former NCC line, in July 1985, to test the impact of heavy trains on sensitive monitoring equipment being installed at the nearby NI Science Park. Here we see GM No 113 and a rake of loaded wagons with GM No 112 at the rear. Who would have guessed that fifteen years later would see steam-hauled ballast trains passing this very location?

To mark the long-awaited reopening to passenger traffic of the Bleach Green to Antrim line in 2001, several special trains were operated between Belfast Central and Antrim. Included was one formed by an 'Enterprise' De Dietrich set, shown here approaching Ballyrobert bridge, about half a mile on the Antrim side of Kingsbog, between Mossley West and Templepatrick loop, with a special from Antrim. The reopened line was built as single track from Monkstown to Antrim but in 2005 NIR conducted a survey of future requirements on the Londonderry line, including new loops, re-doubling, etc.

Representing NIR's first example of new loco purchase in 1969, one must wonder why three small locos with limited availability were chosen, rather than increasing the shortly to be placed Hunslet order to five or six locos with all round availability. Seen at York Road station in June 1984, DH Class No 1 pauses after shunting RPSI stock into the station. Withdrawn by 1989, all three were purchased for static preservation. Nos 2 and 3 have since been shipped to Sri Lanka for further work; in early 2006, No 1 was at Merthyr Tydfil, Wales, being stripped, donating parts to the other two. The steam loco in the background is preserved LMS NCC 2-6-4T No 4.

Twenty years later and York Road station is only a memory. Viewed from a train, and from a more northeasterly direction, GM loco, No 111 *Great Northern*, is stabled in roughly the same location as DH No 1 was in the previous photograph. No 111's train is made up of coaches formerly used on the 'Gatwick Express' service from London Victoria to Gatwick Airport, apart from generator van No 8911, which was new to NIR in 1970 as No 811. It was converted for use with the Gatwick stock in February 2002 and renumbered 8911 at that time.

Due to permanent way work in August 1984, this RPSI special from Whitehead to Bangor via Antrim was hauled by DH No 2 from Greenisland to Whiteabbey, with the steam loco that brought the train from Whitehead providing banking assistance at the rear. At Whiteabbey, the steam loco took the train to Antrim via the emergency crossover at Bleach Green Junction. The DH then returned light to York Road. Once again, a photo such as this would now be impossible as track walking permits are no longer issued and trespass is dealt with severely by Translink and the courts.

70 Class No 72 *River Foyle* leaves Carrickfergus with a stopping train to Belfast in June 1985. The garish livery carried would do some of the present mainland Train Operating Companies proud but it was in fact part of a Sealink promotion for the now-axed, short sea route between Larne and Stranraer. Similarly-liveried Mk1 coaches, hauled by Class 47 diesel locomotives, were operated by British Rail on the connecting service between Stranraer and Glasgow Central. At this time, the Carrickfergus area was still signalled by Belfast and Northern Counties Railway semaphores, with the signal shown, protecting platforms 2 and 3, being a particularly attractive example. No 72 was withdrawn in October 1985.

Multi-purpose diesel (MPD) No 51 is seen approaching Downshire with a Whitehead to Belfast train in September 1979. By this stage, the history of the MPD units was well into the final chapter, with the remaining sets working out their last days on the Larne line and on the short-lived local service between York Road and Antrim via Monkstown. I recall seeing No 64 working as a single unit on an engineering train at Lisahally, outside Derry, in late 1982 or early 1983. No 51 remained in service until February 1980.

Observed here on a gloriously warm and sunny August day in 1983 is 80 Class No 84, approaching Slaughterford bridge north of Whitehead, with an up Belfast train. Now scrapped, No 84 powered the last train from Great Victoria Street in April 1976. Nineteen years later, in September 1995, she also worked the first train from the newly-rebuilt Great Victoria Street station. Her preservation, some might argue, could have symbolised the errors of transport policy between 1976 and 1995 but that was not to be.

During most of 2002 and into 2003, the non-availability of NIR GM locomotives for anything other the Dublin 'Enterprise' and the Newry commuter service led to the use of Irish Rail 'small GM' locos for NIR engineering trains.
No 188, in faded IR orange and black livery, is seen here at Larne Harbour in February 2003 having just arrived with a train of ballast hoppers. The driver is Brian McCarthy.

The MV Class locomotives were not obtained by NIR to work passenger trains, but enthusiast railtours and the Railway Preservation Society of Ireland's 'North Coast Flyer' in 1990 illustrated the versaltility of these capable and robust engines in the twilight of their career. Seen here at Bangor in September 1989, No 104 has run round her train of RPSI stock and waits to take an Irish Traction Group tour to Belfast. Formerly numbered 216 by Irish Rail, No 104 was withdrawn in 1994.

Looking at the multi-engined diesel (MED) units from a 2006 perspective, it is difficult not to agree with the view that these units were modern and very futuristic for their time and would not have been out of place on the railway of 2006. Seen here thirty-one years earlier, in August 1975, is No 34, running in to Carnalea station from the Belfast direction. Withdrawn two years later, No 34 was one of the dozens of railway vehicles subsequently dumped in Crosshill Quarry.

Another August 1975 view, this time of Cultra station with a Bangor train passing. Rush hour traffic on the Bangor line often required two three-car MED units to work in multiple. This might explain the missing flap over the drawgear on MED No 25. When this view was taken, Cultra station had been closed for almost eighteen years. It was reopened in July 1978 and provides convenient access to the adjacent Ulster Folk and Transport Museum. The station building at Cultra is now privately owned and in need of substantial refurbishment.

A 1999 view of a 450 Class set at the leafy Marino station on a Portadown train. The 450 Class units offer similar basic suburban type seating as the MED sets before them but until the arrival of the new CAF units they were seen all over the NIR network. These units are now being repainted from the pale grey and blue with a green stripe, seen here, into an attractive blue and silver scheme. Like the MED units, the 450 Class sets used as many components as possible from older trains.

A spring 2004 picture of General Motors locomotive No 111 *Great Northern* passing Sydenham, with a bridge and platform clearance train made up of former 'Gatwick Express' Mk2 stock. No 111 entered traffic in February 1981 while the 'Gatwick' stock came to Northern Ireland twenty years later. In late afternoon, when this picture was taken, the loco and stock would usually be stabled at Great Victoria Street station prior to working the 1715 commuter service to Newry.

In this picture we see an MED set, led by No 25, arriving at platform 2 at Belfast's Queen's Quay station, having just left the railcar shed. By this stage work was well advanced on the building of the new Central Services Depot on the site of the old yard, with a consequent reduction in track layout. Note the yet to be installed turntable just to the left of the train. The square, white plate below the cab window had a red glass centre and was fitted over the headlight instead of carrying a tail lamp. No 25 was withdrawn in 1978, the former Belfast and County Down station at Queen's Quay having closed to passengers in 1976.

The BCDR's Queen's Quay station was the only terminus in Belfast with locomotive release roads at its main platforms. The site of the lifted road between platforms 2 and 3 is clearly visible in this September 1975 picture. The MED power car (No 32) and trailer lying in the old Holywood bay platform (left) would be used, as required, to strengthen trains. No 34 is at the head of the other set. Note the Bangor line weedkiller train just visible behind the trailer. This comprised a tank on a four-wheel wagon, another four-wheel wagon and a former GNR brake van. This whole site, including the Central Services Depot, is now buried under the eastern approaches to the Lagan road bridge.

An unidentified Hunslet locomotive propels its short train into Belfast Central station from Central Services Depot prior to forming a down service to Londonderry. This picture was captured in September 1984, three years after the Hunslet locomotives had been replaced on the Dublin line by the GM locos. The leading vehicle, Driving Van Trailer No 813, was later used as a standard brake coach and renumbered accordingly. It was withdrawn in 2000.

Not all MED units were 'new build'. A substantial number of power cars and trailers were either rebuilds, or simple conversions, of steam-hauled stock. This led to MED trains made up of both elderly and modern stock with various bodyshape and roof profiles emphasising the origin of the these trains. The two-car set, shown here shortly after Central station opened for Bangor trains in March 1976, differs from the earlier MED sets pictured as both power units are rebuilds from prewar steam-hauled stock. No 23, leading, was withdrawn in 1978.

Some of the differences between 'new build' MED power car No 29, at Belfast Central's platform 3 (left) and a rebuild, No 23, standing at platform 2, are apparent in this April 1976 study.

Awaiting the 'right away' at Central station on 20 October 1979 is Hunslet No 101 *Eagle* hauling the 1430 to Dublin. In the background, at platform 1, an MPD railcar set can be seen having arrived shortly before on the RPSI 'Farewell to the MPDs' railtour from York Road to Bangor and back. Attached to the train was a former GNR dining car. This trip is understood to have been only the second time an MPD set reached Bangor; it was also the last!

For almost thirty years, the three-car 80 Class set was the standard NIR train. Here, a set, headed by Driving Trailer No 753, stands at Botanic station on a sunny August day in 1994. No 753, now renumbered as 8753, dates from 1969 and was originally built as BR coach No 5498. Converted for use in Northern Ireland in 1984, at the time of writing it is still in service. Botanic station opened on 26 April 1976 when the rebuilt line from Belfast Central to Central Junction came into public use.

Hunslet No 101 *Eagle* arrives at City Hospital on a Portadown to Bangor local service shortly after the station opened on 6 October 1986. No 101 entered traffic in July 1970 and is presently stored, engineless, at the RPSI site at Whitehead, Co Antrim. It was last used in July 1993. A short wall on the down platform at City Hospital (behind the train) incorporates in the brickwork an elongated approximation of the British Rail 'double arrow' logo.

The Belfast Central Railway, which linked the former Great Northern and County Down lines, was closed by the UTA in July 1965. At one time the Central line had been busy with GNR goods services from the west, especially cattle trains from Enniskillen bringing live animals to Belfast Docks for shipment to Great Britain. The connection to the GNR main line was at Central Junction, seen here In 1976 just prior to reopening and the subsequent diversion of services from Great Victoria Street station to Belfast Central station. Central Junction proper was reinstated in 1995, with the reopening of Great Victoria Street, and now forms part of a triangular junction. The rail vehicle is an early NIR tamping and lining machine, part of which was later converted to a hedgecutter appropriately numbered HC1.

It's the last day for the old GNR terminus at Great Victoria Street in April 1976 and a two-car 80 Class unit waits at platform 1, better known in GNR days as the motor platform. One of my earliest memories here was seeing an old GNR Kitchen Car, No N166, lying in a short siding adjacent to this platform from about 1966 to 1969. Throughout this period, the same few of what appeared to be eggs were visible at the kitchen window. Then it disappeared, only to reappear a week or two later in NIR all over maroon. Shortly after the repaint, the coach was hauled to Adelaide and scrapped. To the best of my knowledge, it never ran in public service in the maroon livery.

Another view of the old Great Victoria Street station on its last day, 24 April 1976, from the North signal cabin. The roof of a CIÉ Cravens coach, which was being used for clearance runs between Central Junction and Central station, is just visible. Note, on the right-hand side, Murray's tobacco factory, which closed in 2005 and was, sadly, demolished in March 2006. It was a feature of the many photographs taken in the station area.

Seen from a different angle to the classic line-up of Great Northern AEC railcars by R Clements Lyttle in Alan McCutcheon's *Railway History in Pictures, Ireland Volume 2* is a pre-dawn study of two of the stylish, new CAF, or C3K, trains at Great Victoria Street station. Sixty-nine vehicles are made up into 23 three-car sets which see use across the entire NIR network. As built, the 'new' Great Victoria had short platforms which were extended within a few years to accommodate 'Enterprise' workings. The 'join' in platforms 3/4 is clearly visible!

During 2005, the first 450 Class units were outshopped in the attractive blue and silver livery applied to the CAF units. Looking pristine in June of that year is No 8452 *Olderfleet Castle*, resting at platform 3 at Great Victoria Street. The nine 450 Class units were built between October 1985 and June 1987 on British Rail Mk1 coach underframes. Eight were originally powered with engines recovered from withdrawn 70 Class units, the ninth engine coming from damaged 80 Class No 88.

A classic study of a four-car, high power to weight ratio, Londonderry train passing Adelaide, taken shortly after the leading power car, No 99, had entered service in June 1978. Seen in the cab, on the fireman's side, a phrase still used by NIR drivers even on the new C3K railcars, is York Road inspector Frank Dunlop who in many ways personified the character of the old railway and in so doing commanded great respect from staff. An NCC man to the bone, he is now enjoying retirement in Carrickfergus. No 99 was the last 80 Class power car to be delivered and was named *Sir Myles Humphries* in September 1978. She is now withdrawn.

Another view at Adelaide showing an 80 Class driving trailer heading a Lisburn local into the station. Note that this set is made up of a Suburban-liveried Driving Trailer and Driving Motor Brake Standard (power car) and a red and grey Trailer Standard. Combinations of the various livery schemes was not unusual. It was at Adelaide back in late 1968 that Jim Edgar and myself unsuccessfully attempted to light up and steam withdrawn GNR locos UG Class No 49 and SG3 Class No 37!

Finaghy was the location in the late 1960s for many hours of closely observing trains, another favoured spot being the now-closed accommodation crossing on the Belfast side of the station. When this picture was taken in early 1984 80 Class No 85, heading a southbound train through the suburban station, was already nine years old. She is now withdrawn. The summer smell of cresote-covered timbers is now also a memory and the frequently-vandalised station is a much less pleasant place.

An 80 Class set, headed by No 91, passes through the M1 tunnel, towards Black's Road bridge in April 1988. The motorway was promised in the 1960s to replace the Derry Road railway but it never got beyond Dungannon. The closure of the railway did not encourage our family to use the new, grey and red UTA 'Wolfhound' express coaches to visit Omagh but, rather, encouraged my father to purchase a green 1964 Ford Cortina, registration number 530 RZ. In early 2006, No 91, new in February 1978, is stored and is unlikely to run again.

Seen here at Dunmurry in May 1984 are two 70 Class power cars en route from York Road to Central Services Depot. The degraded track over which the train is travelling was little more than ten years old and its condition emphasises the importance of maintenance and asset management. The former stationmaster here, John Haskins, lived nearby and can only have been relieved when the GNR station building he looked after in the 1960s was demolished, such was the vandalism. John died early in 2006.

In the early 1960s, we often visited my grandmother at Dunmurry and used the bus to get there. On the journey home to Finaghy in the evening, the Somerville family would wait at the UTA bus stop, opposite Jim Chambers' newsagents shop – all except me, as I would be standing by the railway, at Meeting House Crossing, hoping to see a train. On one such occasion, I recall seeing a heavy, steam-hauled goods train with either an NCC Mogul or Jeep struggle past en route probably to Portadown or Strabane. In an attempt to recreate the scene some twenty-one years later, in 1985, we see 80 Class No 93 approach the crossing with a Lisburn local. No 93 is now withdrawn.

With the characteristic roar of a General Motors engine in full flight, Irish Rail loco No 071 shakes the foundations at Hilden as she passes with an up Dublin express in Spring 1995. The performance of these powerful locos (2475 hp), with trains of perhaps twelve coaches, was outstanding. This loco was on hire to Northern Ireland Railways due to the poor availability of its own GM locos.

Towards the end of their lives, the 70 Class units were likely to appear on any train. Despite its Sealink livery, intended for Belfast to Larne Harbour workings, this three-car set, powered by No 72 *River Foyle,* was no exception and here we see it leaving Lisburn on a Bangor working in May 1984. This colourful ensemble looked rather incongruous with the traditional GNR signalling in the station.

Carrying the original, attractive maroon, cream and orange livery of 1985 is 450 Class No 458 *Antrim Castle*, leaving Lisburn on a Portadown train in early 1989. In the distance is the former GNR good shed where, in 1966, Glover Compound No 85, minus tender, and an old GNR coach, still in GNR livery, awaited discovery by the same intrepid pair of railway enthusiasts who were later to try and light up two withdrawn steam locos lying in Adelaide yard (see page 44). The old shed is now demolished but the Glover Compound still exists in preservation; pity about that lovely coach though.

A Derry to Belfast train, formed of a three-car 80 Class set, is seen here on the third line between Knockmore halt and Lisburn. This line was brought into use in May 1977 following a lengthy planning dispute between local residents and NIR. I have never understood the need for its construction; a simple junction at Knockmore, controlled from Lisburn, would, in my view, have sufficed. Knockmore halt, with its staggered platforms, was situated by the bridge and was unusual in that it was served in the up direction by Portadown trains and in the down direction by the much less frequent Londonderry line service. The site of the former Knockmore Junction was about ¾mile beyond the bridge.

A rare picture of 80 Class No 88, seen at Crumlin on a northbound Antrim train in September 1980. This power car was the first 80 Class to be withdrawn, following a rear end collision at Hilden in March 1983 in which driver Herbie Dean was killed. No 88's engine now powers No 459 *Killyleagh Castle*.

This view, taken from inside MED No 10, of MPD No 42 at the former airfield at Nutts Corner, near Crumlin, as both await their final fate, dates from September 1980. MEDs Nos 10, 19 and 21 and MPDs Nos 39, 42 and 62 were used at this location as sheds from 1978 (No 62 from 1977) to 1980. From Nutts Corner the remains were taken to Crosshill Quarry for disposal. No 10 had been built in 1952 and was last used in 1977. No 42, a conversion from coach No 341 in 1957, had last worked in 1975.

A Londonderry to Belfast Central train passes the disused Aldergrove halt (closed 1960), between Antrim and Crumlin, in May 1981, with No 77 *River Braid* leading. This area has long been the centre of speculation regarding a link to the nearby Belfast International Airport.

We now return to Lisburn to begin the last part of this Rail Runabout over NIR metals and on to Dundalk. Seen here, in this late 1970s picture, is Hunslet loco No 103 *Merlin*. Trainee driver Noel Playfair, with long hair, can be seen seated on the fireman's side. By this stage, the performance of the Hunslet locomotives on the daily runs to and from Dublin was poor and the new 111 Class locos, two of which were on order, were shortly to take over. No 103 was withdrawn in 1989 and broken up in Ballymena at 1997. Noel is now driving trains and is a popular member of the small team who man RPSI steam trains.

The mid 1990s saw much-needed investment in the Belfast to Dublin service. Northern Ireland Railways obtained two new locomotives, similar to the Irish Rail 201 Class locos, and placed them in service before the new stock arrived in 1997. Painted in the intervening period in an attractive dark blue livery, similar to the earlier GM locos, No 208 *River Lagan* is seen at Lisburn with a Sunday service from Dublin. At this time the station was undergoing substantial refurbishment.

Driver Bob Gilmore is seen here at the controls of GM loco No 112 *Northern Counties* ready to leave Lisburn in 1985. Beyond, CIÉ loco No 018 can be seen approaching with a goods for Adelaide. No 112 is now on long term loan to Irish Rail and is understood to be a reliable machine. Sadly, Bob Gilmore died in 2000.

Now only a memory in this area but in 1975 they represented the future. Sporting the red and grey livery is this three-car 80 Class set on a Belfast to Portadown working, approaching the site of the long-closed Knockmore Junction in August 1984. In the far distance, an RPSI steam train has just passed Knockmore halt as it approaches Lisburn. Knockmore halt is now closed although a major new park and ride station is under consideration for the Knockmore area as part of long term plans.

Damhead station closed in July 1973, which explains its run down appearance as this southbound goods, with CIÉ 001 Class loco No 034 and a rake of fertiliser and cement empties, passes through. Occasionally, this train carried Richardson's fertiliser southbound. The waiting shelter on the down platform was typical GNR and it was sad to see it decay after closure. A few similar shelters are still in use on Irish Rail.

For many years, as the world and the railway continued to change, Moira station was a pleasant place to while away an afternoon with a visit to the signal cabin for a wee bit of craic and a cup of very strong tea; there was always a welcome guaranteed and the Great Northern influence was all around. It was on the day of one such visit, in May 1982, that this Dublin to Belfast express, with GM No 112 *Northern Counties* in charge, was photographed. In 2006, the old wheel-operated level crossing gates have gone, the cabin is also closed, but interestingly relocated and preserved on a strange elevated site behind the up platform, and the station is busier than ever.

Metro-Vick No 106 rests at Portadown engineering sidings in 1994. One of a small batch of secondhand locos purchased by NIR in the mid 1980s, they were used primarily on permanent way trains. Withdrawn in 1995, this loco reverted to its former CIÉ identity after being purchased for preservation at Cahirciveen. More recently, it was badly damaged, as a result of vandalism, and may have to be scrapped.

Scarcely a mile of NIR can be travelled over without some reminder of a time when the railway played a much greater role in society than it does today. Consumer demand for just in time products, the point to point advantage of car travel and the growing impact of the internet on the need to travel all have, or will determine the shape of the railway in the future. Portadown was a major railway junction in its heyday and it is here where I believe the next decade will see a modest revival if demographics, property prices and traffic congestion continue to grow on the Armagh corridor. Here we see an 80 Class set, with No 85 leading, leaving Portadown with a Sham Fight special to Scarva in July 1994.

Seen here outside Portadown in July 1994 is a nine-car 80 Class set, headed by No 84, running wrong line from Scarva. To allow such workings on the up line, and to ensure the safety of passengers and railway staff, this track is treated as a temporary single line section and trains carry a pilotman, even though both tracks are now signalled for bi-directional operation. The practice of running the annual Scarva specials wrong line has been in place since steam days.

The NIR 'Rail Runabout' ticket allowed travel on CIÉ metals as far as Dundalk and with this town being the spiritual home for the, dare I say it, finest and most enterprising railway in Ireland, it seems somehow right to bring our journey to an end with this view of an up 'Enterprise Express' working passing Dundalk Central cabin in August 1986. Appropriately, it is hauled by GM No 111 *Great Northern*!